Oh, Behave!

Manners in the Community

Siân Smith

Chicago, Illinois

www.capstonepub.com
Visit our website to find out
more information about
Heinemann-Raintree books.

To order:

☎ Phone 800-747-4992

💻 Visit www.capstonepub.com
to browse our catalog and order online.

Edited by Dan Nunn, Rebecca Rissman, and John-Paul Wilkins
Designed by Marcus Bell
Picture research by Elizabeth Alexander
Production by Alison Parsons
Originated by Capstone Global Library Ltd
Printed and bound in China by Leo Paper Products Ltd

16 15 14 13 12
10 9 8 7 6 5 4 3 2 1

Library of Congress Cataloging-in-Publication Data
Smith, Siân.
 Oh, behave! : manners in the community / Siân Smith.—1st ed.
  p. cm.
 Includes bibliographical references and index.
 ISBN 978-1-4329-6639-3 (hb)—ISBN 978-1-4329-6644-7 (pb)
1. Manners and customs—Juvenile literature. I. Title.
GT85.S65 2013
390—dc23
                        2011049834

Acknowledgments
We would like to thank the following for permission to reproduce
photographs: © Capstone Publishers pp. 9, 10, 19, 22, 23 (Karon
Dubke); Alamy pp. 16, 23 (© Cultura Creative), 18, 22 (© SFL
Travel); Corbis pp. 5 (© moodboard), 7 (© Steve Hix/Somos
Images), 8 (© Yosuke Tanaka/Aflo), 14 (© Jim Craigmyle); Getty
Images pp. 11 (i love images/Cultura), 15 (Fuse); iStockphoto pp.
13 (© nautilus_shell_studios), 17 (© charlybutcher), 20 (© Rich
Legg), 21 (© Steve Debenport); Shutterstock pp. 4 (© Monkey
Business Images), 6 (© greenland), 12, 22 (© Ilya Andriyanov).

Front cover photograph of girl emptying cereal package in a
supermarket reproduced with permission of Photolibrary (i love
images). Rear cover photograph of boy throwing away trash
reproduced with permission of iStockphoto (© charlybutcher).

Every effort has been made to contact copyright holders
of material reproduced in this book. Any omissions will be
rectified in subsequent printings if notice is given to the
publisher.

We would like to thank Nancy Harris and Dee Reid for their
assistance in the preparation of this book.

Contents

Good Manners .4

Show People Your Manners 6

Special Places 14

Everywhere You Go 16

Best Behavior 22

Picture Glossary 23

Index 24

Good Manners

People with good manners know how to behave in different places.

If you have good manners, people will enjoy taking you out.

Show People Your Manners

Don't be rude when you speak
to people.

Say "please" and "thank you" when you ask for something.

Don't sit down if someone needs a seat more than you.

Ask if the person would like your seat.

Don't push in front of people.

Wait your turn.

Don't pick your nose.

Use a tissue to wipe your nose.

Special Places

It is important to talk quietly in some places.

It is important not to touch things in some places.

Everywhere You Go

litter

Never drop litter. Litter spoils places for everyone.

Put litter in a trash can.

Don't put your feet on seats.

It will make them dirty for everyone.

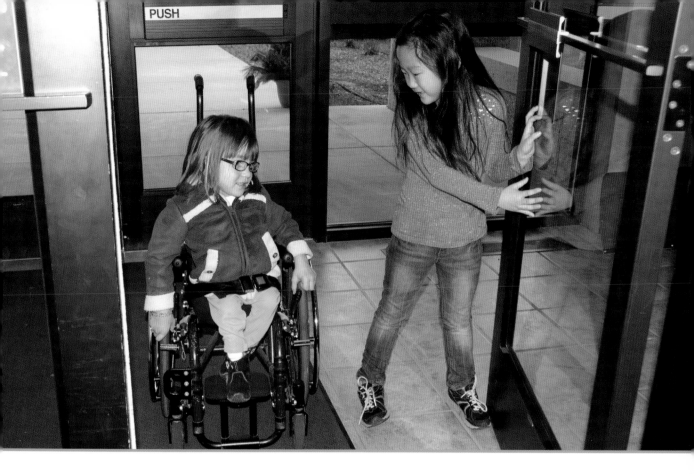

Hold doors open for other people.

Treat people the way you want to be treated.

People with good manners make the
world a nicer place to be.

Best Behavior

Which person here has good manners?

Answer on page 24

Picture Glossary

good manners ways of behaving politely and well

litter trash

Index

good manners 4,
  5, 21

litter 16, 17

quiet 14

rude 6

tissue 13

Answer to question on page 22
The girl holding the door open for someone
has good manners.

Notes for parents and teachers
Before reading
Explain that good manners are ways of behaving—they help us to understand what to do and
how to act. They are important because they show us how to treat each other and help us to
get along well with other people. What examples of good manners can the children think of?
List these together.

After reading
- Ask the children to share examples of good manners and bad manners they've seen when they have
  been out to different places. For any examples of bad manners, discuss together what that person
  should have done.
- Tell the children to imagine they are organizing a school trip (this could be for younger pupils). Divide
  the children into groups and ask each group to decide where they will go. Ask them to think about
  how the children they take will need to behave. Each group can decide what good manners tips they
  would give to the children on the trip.
- Give pairs or groups of children examples of good manners when out and about to role-play. Different
  groups can try this at the same time, or groups could take turns and be given more support. Children
  can guess what is being shown and think about how the people in the role-play would feel.